The Road to the Aisle

The Road to the Aisle

GILLEAN MACLEAN

SAINT ANDREW PRESS
Edinburgh

Revised edition published in 2009 by
SAINT ANDREW PRESS
121 George Street, Edinburgh EH2 4YN

ISBN 978 0 7152 0926 4

This book is a new and original text but Saint Andrew Press and the author would like
to acknowledge James Martin, for his work as author of an earlier book of the same name
published by Saint Andrew Press in 1972.

British Library Cataloguing in Publication Data
A catalogue record for this book is available from the British Library

It is the Publisher's policy to only use papers that are natural and recyclable and that have
been manufactured from timber grown in renewable, properly managed forests. All of
the manufacturing processes of the papers are expected to conform to the environmental
regulations of the country of origin.

Typeset in Bembo by Waverley Typesetters, Fakenham
Printed and bound in the United Kingdom by Mackay & Inglis, Glasgow

Contents

Dear both,

This wee book is designed to help you negotiate the Scottish 'Road to the Aisle'. It is by no means comprehensive for there will always be differences of practice depending on the minister and church you have chosen for your special day. I am a Church of Scotland minister and have approached the subject from my own experience of conducting many weddings, each one of them unique. One of the riches of the Church of Scotland is to be found in its variety.

Indeed, it is possible that you are coming at this from different branches or denominations of the Church _in_ Scotland and will be trying to accommodate that within your service. You will find, I hope, that most ministers or priests will bend over backwards to make your day as memorable and as significant as they can. We Scots are nothing if not inventive.

Above all, enjoy it.

> May I wish you God's blessing
> for your forthcoming marriage
> and in your life together.

GILLEAN MACLEAN

Making the Arrangements

So you're getting married? Congratulations are in order of course, but I'd like to begin with a bit of a health warning. A wedding doesn't need to cost a fortune, despite what the magazines and advertisers say, and the photographer, dressmaker, kilt-hire establishment, cake-maker, florist, hotelier and even the prospective in-laws (important as all of these are to the day) are **not** in charge. Your marriage is between two people who love each other and who cannot contemplate not being together to the extent that they want to make public their feelings for each other and commit themselves to a lifetime together.

It's an important step, and one that sometimes involves a couple's own children. A lot of people stand to be upset and disappointed if things go awry. Remember that if you're not sure about any of the arrangements or if it looks like they will cause significant strife then please take your time. It is much better to postpone for a little while rather than to enter into a huge expense and find it impossible to back out of or cancel if things get difficult.

The Place

In Scotland a couple can get married at a location of their choice, and many people are very inventive. Your parish minister is allowed to conduct marriages in hotels, on beaches, up mountains and in private homes (as well as in the Church they serve of course).

However, most ministers find that it is not only convenient and appropriate but sensible to use the parish church. Only there can they be sure that all the elements of the service are attended to according to their own practice. If you have a request regarding the venue then by all means discuss it with your minister but do be aware that for a number of reasons your request may not be possible. Indeed, some ministers have a definite policy on this and will only agree to conduct services in the church building. However, since April 2002 a change in policy in Scotland now allows **registrars** to conduct marriages in the couple's choice of location, although this does incur an additional cost and as you are now reading this booklet I must assume that you have chosen a Christian marriage. Registrars will conduct a beautifully sensitive service but do not allow music or readings that have any religious content whatsoever.

A Christian marriage service is not just a contract between two people before witnesses. The vows that are exchanged are done solemnly and in the presence of God. I think you'll agree that we need all the help we can get when it comes to relationships. With the Holy Spirit as the third member of your partnership it is my prayer that you will have a long and very fulfilling life together.

IF YOU HAVE BEEN MARRIED IN A CIVIL CEREMONY AND WISH TO HAVE A MARRIAGE BLESSING AT A LATER DATE IN CHURCH IT IS USUALLY POSSIBLE TO DO SO BY ARRANGEMENT WITH YOUR LOCAL MINISTER; THE SAME APPLIES FOR RENEWAL OF VOWS AT AN EVEN LATER DATE.

Which Church?

Many people choose the church they wish to be married in to fit in with the location of their reception venue, or because it has a pleasing aspect. While this is understandable and indeed sensible from a practical point of view, it does not necessarily fit in with the practice of the parish minister. It is customary for one or other of the partners to have some connection with the church in question. It may be that one of you is a member or have parents or grandparents that are members, or you may simply live within the bounds of the parish. If you do not fulfil these criteria then please do still contact the minister with your request. Most ministers are very happy to be part of your special day and to welcome all to their church.

If you are a member of a church in another location and wish your own minister to travel to conduct or share in the service then make sure that he or she is able to give of their time, that there is accommodation arranged for them locally and that they are offered travelling expenses for their trip. Ministers do not get paid extra for the number of services they conduct and they are generally busy people so may not be able to help with a wedding unless someone else is arranged to stand in for them, and this too incurs a cost to their congregation.

If this is your wish, it will have to be discussed with the parish minister in the church of your choice, and his or her permission granted.

If you are not members or attenders of the church in question it is a good idea (and certainly won't do you any harm) to go along on one or two Sundays before you make your final decision. Ministers vary in their practice and it will familiarise you with how things are done in that particular church. You will find, too, that the congregation are delighted to have in their midst a prospective wedding couple. It is important that you begin your married life in a place that you love and are comfortable with, and that your service will be one that reflects your own level of faith and belief. If in any doubt please do call the minister and discuss things with her or him. Their contact details or those of their clerk are often on the notice-board of the church or in the telephone book. Many churches nowadays also have web pages you can consult and these may give further guidance on the arrangements for marriages.

The Date and Time of the Wedding

Once you have the venue and minister chosen then it is time to fix the date and time. This is a matter for consultation between reception venue and church. Some churches may have many couples to fit in to a day and will have defined times for services. In my own parish we usually fit in with the timings of ferries so that guests can get there in good time and get home again on the same day if they wish. In one previous charge, those who had timed their wedding around the times of our local football club's fixtures had to arrange alternative routes for guests if they were not to get stuck for the duration of the service in football traffic.

Thinking this through carefully at this stage is well worth doing and can avoid any later complications or unnecessary stresses on the day. It may be a good idea to provide a map for those who are not sure of the location of the church. You could include any special instructions along with it. **But please do not make any irrevocable decisions regarding time and place until you have a firm decision from the minister of your chosen church.** We do occasionally take holidays and those who are filling in for us may not be qualified to conduct a wedding. There have been times when a couple has consulted me complete with date, time and other venues arranged, right down to the flowers and photographer, and I have had to tell them that I am unable to conduct their service because I am already engaged elsewhere.

Charges, Church-officers and Tunes

There are other people who may well be involved in your special day, and some of them will need to be consulted at an early point in the discussions. Money will also have to change hands, although churches vary in that respect. There is usually a set fee for the use of the building and for the services of the musician and the church-officer. Your minister will guide you in this respect.

It is as well to make sure that fees are paid in advance of the service because in the hustle and bustle of the day sometimes things get forgotten. No-one enjoys chasing people for money after the event, and churches are no exception to the rule.

Perhaps this might be a job for a best man or bridesmaid or someone who has not got a role as yet in the proceedings? The parish minister conducts your wedding as part of his or her calling. They should not exact a fee from you. If you feel the need to offer a 'thank you' gift then that is entirely voluntary, vouchers or tokens of some sort are often the best.

The **church-officer** is the person who will make sure the building is warm and comfortable and open when required. He or she is also the best person to contact if you need access for florists or advice on any matter to do with decoration, seating and the logistics of the day. Flowers for the church can be a big expense so you may wish to consider doing some of this yourself – the church-officer can usually give advice on local florists or members of the church who could help.

If any of your party has a disability that needs to be accommodated please mention it so that their comfort can be taken into account.

Most churches have an organ or piano and a **musician** who plays for them. Speak to the musician, along with the minister, about your choices of music and your thoughts on what might be appropriate, and particularly if you have any special requests in this regard. It is always difficult to choose music for a special occasion but unless you are very sure and have already made your choice then there are plenty of people who can help. Most music outlets and some department stores have a selection of CDs for sale which have been compiled especially with weddings in mind. You can spend some time listening to one to help you choose something that suits. Most organists will be happy to comply with your requests if they are not too outlandish.

Please remember that they are the experts and they will know what will sound best on their particular instrument. Something simple played well and with feeling may well be better than a very complicated and less popular tune.

As far as hymns go, there are a number that are well-known as 'wedding' hymns and in many hymn-books they are grouped together. There are some lovely new ones around but bear in mind that if you are the only one who knows the song, this is not the day to launch your solo singing career.

Some churches will allow **recorded music** during the ceremony but they have to have a special licence for this so do check in advance. If there is to be a video of the service then usually there is an additional charge to cover the recording of the music.

Pipers can be a great asset to any wedding and you may wish to be 'piped in' or out. You will need to book your piper well in advance and make sure the church and organist knows that he or she will be there. Some churches will allow the piper to play inside the church building but others do not, often because they are simply too small to accommodate the volume. I remember vividly an elderly lady telling me she had suffered from tinnitus for six months after a local piper played a lament during one of our funeral services.

If you are not using the church building because your minister has agreed to marry you in another location then it is your job to make sure that the venue is suitably laid out and that the musician is engaged in good time. It is a good policy to put the organiser and the musician in touch with the minister so that all will go smoothly on the day. Your minister may want to have a look at the arrangements before then and will almost certainly arrange some kind of rehearsal, regardless of the venue chosen. It's always a good idea to run through things in the location where they are going to take place. Some alarming last-minute hitches have been ironed out at wedding rehearsals on the very eve of the wedding. On one occasion, a couple turned up for the rehearsal the day before the wedding was to take place and had not communicated with the registrar at all. It being a bank holiday the office was closed. Luckily, we were able to find the registrar at home who very kindly got everything organised for us just in the nick of time. Leaving things this late is not to be recommended – more about registrars later.

A final thought. Although it's an exciting time for everyone, it's not always a good idea to bring your entire family to the rehearsal. This is definitely a case of 'too many cooks spoiling the broth'. Only those who are going to be taking part need come along. Bride, groom, attendants, close family and anyone who is reading or playing an instrument may wish to be present.

The Marriage Service

I t has always been important to me that each marriage service is one that is personal and memorable. Different denominations, and even different ministers within the same branch of the Church will have differing styles but most ministers will want to discuss the ceremony with you both over a couple of meetings if that is possible.

If you simply want to book the venue and turn up on the day then you will have little or no say in what happens and your service will lack the personal touch that will make your wedding really memorable.

Some ministers will have a set service they like to follow (or one that they are required to use by their denomination), although even within that there are elements that can be altered to suit, and other sections where you can have an input.

Vows

What form do you wish these to take? Do you simply want to say 'I do' in response to the minister's question or do you want to speak the words of the vows to each other? I personally prefer the latter, even if it does occasionally result in a few emotional tears. Don't worry, whatever you choose you will not have to memorise anything. The minister will guide you through it all. She or he is the only one who can really make a mistake.

Readings

What would you like to have read during the service? The minister will usually include at least one Bible reading but it may also be possible to choose another reading, poetry or prose, that may be special to you.

All of these things, having been chosen earlier, can be run through at the rehearsal.

The Wedding Day

Perhaps the best way of getting to grips with the whole thing is for me to run through what might be the way of things if I was to be the minister conducting your wedding.

Having been involved as the mother of the bride myself, I know just how chaotic it can be on the morning of your special day. Flowers to be collected, clothes to be pressed, hair to be done, cars to be organised, dogs to be farmed out, cakes to be collected and delivered. Before the day, make a checklist and do as many of these things as possible in advance. Pass on whatever you can to **reliable** other people.

Arriving at the Church

The first people to arrive may well be the ushers. They should be there in good time, about an hour before the service, as many people like to arrive nice and early on the day. The ushers will be able to get to grips with the organisation for seating everyone and make sure all is well. They should always make sure that there are enough seats reserved at the front of the church for the family of the bride and groom and for anyone arriving with the wedding party who will need to have a seat. They should have with them the orders of service, if any, unless they have been delivered to the church the day before, and give the minister enough copies for the bridal party.

The groom and best man should plan to arrive a good half an hour before the service, if only to calm the minister's nerves! I always feel better when they have arrived and I can check that the

rings are in a safe place and that the Marriage Schedule is in order. Only once have I had to send the best man rushing back to the hotel for that all-important piece of paper. It was an anxious twenty minutes, for **without this document the wedding couldn't go ahead. (See Appendix 1.)**

Before the arrival of the bride and when everyone is seated and ready, I will normally have a word with folk about mobile phones and other electronic gadgets. I will also have spoken to anyone who is taking photographs and reminded the congregation not to use their cameras until after the ceremony. I usually give them all a chance to take a photograph at the end but that may not be the case in all churches.

The bridesmaids will be the next to arrive, followed by the bride and the person who is to accompany her down the aisle. This might be her father or brother or a friend. The groom and best man may

have been mingling with guests or hiding nervously in the vestry reading the latest copy of our church magazine but at this point they will be positioned at the front of the assembled congregation, ready to receive the bridal party.

Having said all this, it is by no means inappropriate for bride and groom to arrive together and proceed in this manner down the aisle. If this is what you prefer, please talk to your minister.

When the bride arrives, I usually go to the door for a brief word of reassurance and then when the chosen piece of music begins to play I lead the party in to join the groom.

In Scotland, it is customary for the groom to gaze stoically at whatever is in front of him and not to turn around until his bride is by his side but there are other traditions that can be followed, and some men just can't wait to get a sight of their loved one in all her finery.

The bride is brought to stand on the groom's left-hand side and the person who is accompanying her will be invited to take their seat.

The Service

(I HAVE INCLUDED A TYPICAL ORDER OF SERVICE IN THE APPENDICES AT THE BACK OF THE BOOK.)

The assembled company being welcomed, the first hymn or song will be sung. There follows a statement about marriage, a prayer and then a Bible reading. (This may be one you have chosen for the day or you may have left it up to the minister.)

The congregation will then be invited to stand for the exchange of vows. (This is a good idea, for if they're standing they are less likely to be chatting about the dress or flowers or minister's hairstyle – you would be surprised just how badly behaved wedding guests can be.)

You will be asked to turn and face each other, after of course handing the wedding bouquet to someone else to take care of, and removing any veil.

As far as I know, there are no rules about who articulates their vows first but it is customarily the groom. I will say the words of the vows slowly for each of you to repeat and then ask the best man for the rings.

This can be a hazardous moment. I must say, I do not recommend any fancy arrangements at this point unless they have been well-rehearsed. Small children with stage fright carrying cushions and rings secured by slippery ribbons can have disastrous consequences, and the story of the couple who wanted their rings delivered by owls makes my blood run cold with foreboding.

The rings having been satisfactorily exchanged and placed on the third finger of the left hand (I usually remind both partners which finger it is), I will now declare you to be husband and wife and you will be invited to kiss.

It is worth saying that nerves and heat and all sorts of things can make fingers swell up a little so please do not try to cram a ring on so hard that your partner's finger is close to breaking. This can be sorted out discreetly during the next reading or prayer.

As far as the kiss is concerned, it should probably not last too long. There's plenty of time for more of that later. I remember one Argentine bridegroom who, so relieved and happy to have reached this stage of the wedding service, rushed around kissing everyone, men and women, me included, and had to be restrained by the best man.

After the declaration and kiss, some congregations may break into a spontaneous round of applause. At this stage, I will ask them to be seated and offer a blessing for the bride and groom (you may wish to kneel for this, although I have noticed that this is easier in some dresses than others – hooped underskirts can be somewhat difficult to manage and potentially revealing).

There are usually prayers said for your future happiness and possibly another reading. This is a good place for a piece of poetry or prose read by a friend or member of the family. It is my custom also to offer some words of encouragement or advice to the newly married couple before the second hymn is sung.

At the conclusion of the hymn, the worship service comes to an end with a blessing for all present and then they are invited to be seated for the signing of the register.

NOTE: SOME DENOMINATIONS MAY INCLUDE A CELEBRATION OF THE EUCHARIST/COMMUNION AS PART OF THE WEDDING SERVICE. PLEASE DISCUSS THIS WITH YOUR MINISTER OR PRIEST.

The Schedule

(PLEASE SEE APPENDIX 1 FOR DETAILS OF THE CIVIL REQUIREMENTS FOR A MARRIAGE.)

I like the signing to be in full view of the congregation although some churches will take you out to an office or vestry where this will happen. In either case, it is a good idea to have a piece of music played or some other musical diversion while we are attending to the signing otherwise guests may start to get restless.

You are guided through this by the minister who is required by the registrar to use a pen containing indelible ink. If you are not used to a fountain pen then take care, they can be volatile and you don't want ink anywhere except on the schedule and in the right place.

The bride, groom, minister and two witnesses all sign the form and it is then placed in its envelope to be returned to the registrar within three working days.

This form is very important. Someone reliable must take care of it and make sure it gets back to the registrar in good time. Your marriage must be registered within three working days or potentially you might have to do it all over again!

The photographer will want to have a few pictures of you as you sign, or to set it up for a photograph after we are finished with the formalities. It is at this point that I usually allow the congregation to take a few pictures if they wish, and before it turns into a rabble I will invite the organist to begin playing the music you have chosen for this point in the service and lead the wedding party out into the sunshine (well, hope is one of the great Christian virtues, is it not?).

Confetti, Rice and Other Marital Missiles

Some venues just don't like confetti so please check. It can be messy and difficult to get rid of before the next event, which may not be as festive as your wedding. However, rice is a nice alternative. It is biodegradable and can supply the local birds with a wedding treat. I believe it is possible to buy confetti made from rice paper, which will do the same thing, but do be warned the dye in some confettis can become a permanent feature of your finery if the weather is at all damp.

The practice of throwing money for local children (the 'scramble') is no longer advised for safety reasons.

If you are planning to throw your bouquet at some point for your best single friend to catch then remember you will want it for photographs so best to keep this for later on.

The Reception

This part of the day can become horribly expensive and it doesn't need to be. Think carefully about how many people you would like to have there for the whole event, including any meal you have decided to have. It needn't be a formal sit-down affair, a buffet can work just as well, as long as there is plenty of informal seating available. For many couples, it works best to have close friends and family for the early part of the day and then a larger number of guests for the evening reception. The only tricky thing is trying to keep track of who's who. If you are using a hotel rather than a hall or function room there is usually someone who deals with wedding parties and who can advise you on menus and the order of proceedings.

As photographs can take rather a long time it is advisable to make sure that guests know exactly when they are expected to arrive at the reception and make sure that there is someone to greet them and offer them some refreshments while they wait.

When the photographs are completed, it is usual for the bride and groom to cut the cake although at some weddings this now happens after the meal is over and before the coffee is served. It is entirely up to you.

In Scotland, it has been a tradition for ministers to be the chairperson for the meal and speeches but this is not always possible or appropriate, particularly if you do not know your officiating minister very well or they are not available to come along to the reception. It is perfectly possible that they may have another wedding to conduct or some other business to attend to. If you particularly want to invite your minister then please do so well in advance. They will not be in the least offended if you choose not to.

The hotel will usually appoint someone to guide you through the proceedings. Check if this is the case. If it is not, sit down with those who are going to speak during the reception and write down the order you want things done in. Appoint someone who is good at these things and perhaps has no other role to attend to and can take time to make sure it goes to plan.

There need not be any set order for seating but if you are providing a sit-down meal in a formal or semi-formal setting then it is best to be organised about it. The 'top' table should have the bride and groom at the centre, flanked by their best man and maid and then parents or special guests at either end. If the minister and his or her partner is attending then they may be seated elsewhere and can easily be called upon if you wish them to say a prayer before the meal begins. If this is the case, make sure they know what is required of them and let the master of ceremonies know where they will be sitting.

It seems to be common parlance these days to include a disposable camera on tables to allow guests to take informal photographs during the reception. These can be exchanged and enjoyed later. The practice of delivering 'favours' to special guests is something that has survived the test of time. (These are little gifts, sometimes sugared almonds or other sweets, that are nicely wrapped and delivered as treats, for example to great-grannies or special aunties.)

Speeches

If there are to be toasts and speeches then decide on who and when and let the master of ceremonies (MC) know. It usually goes something like this. The MC begins, with a toast to the bride and groom, followed by the groom who will toast and thank the bridesmaids. The best man will then read any messages or cards that have been received. It is always a good idea to read all messages through in advance just to make sure that they are 'suitable' for the youngest and the oldest of your guests. If they are not, they can always be edited. The best man then follows with a speech, usually containing some 'funnies' about the groom. Please check with your best man that these are not too risqué, there's no point in falling out with anyone at this stage in the proceedings. The groom usually makes a speech too. This need only be brief and should begin with words such as 'on behalf of my wife and myself'. Having said those words it is hardly necessary to say much more and everyone will be suitably charmed. A gift is sometimes presented at this point to the bridesmaids and the best man and also the two 'mothers' (the mother of the bride and the mother of the groom).

However, it is not without precedent for the bride to make some kind of speech and for one or both of the sets of parents to say something too. Regardless of how many there are to be, instruct everyone to keep it brief and make sure you have a definite order of proceedings.

Evening Reception

There are different traditions in different parts of Scotland, for instance in the north-east it is customary to begin the evening reception and ceilidh with a 'grand march'. The wedding couple lead off and are joined by their attendants and then the rest of the company as they parade around the room. In other places the evening is kicked off by the bridal couple leading in the first waltz. It is entirely up to you how you want to play things but if most of your guests are from outside Scotland and you want to have ceilidh dancing then it is a good idea to engage a band that has a 'caller', i.e. someone who will teach the dances as they go along. Otherwise the chaos can be quite alarming and not a little dangerous!

Just remember in all of this that it is your choice what happens at the reception. Don't feel that you have to be tied to any one formula. As long as it is well organised in advance and someone is in charge of the order of proceedings it should be an enjoyable evening for all concerned.

It is a good idea to provide something to eat towards the end of the evening. Coffee and some nibbles will help to soak up any high spirits that are around and avoid unpleasant after-effects. Although there should always be plenty of soft drinks available and cold water too, particularly if there is to be ceilidh dancing.

Afterwards

This is the part where the piper has to be paid, I'm afraid. However, if you have taken my advice you will have made sure that some, at least, of the bills have been paid in advance. If there is anything left outstanding then settle it up as soon as possible so that it doesn't get forgotten. In past times there were all sorts of rules about who pays for what; this has largely been overridden now by necessity. They do say that necessity is the mother of invention! Many couples are paying for their wedding day themselves without input from parents or other family.

As with everything else, it is down to organisation. As long as everyone knows who is responsible for what, well in advance, then it should all run very smoothly. Some couples like to organise the sending of a piece of wedding cake to friends or family that could not attend and then the remainder of the cake is stored away in anticipation of the first christening. (This is less common than it used to be and is not any longer expected, it is up to you to decide whether it is a nice touch you wish to include or not.)

When I got married, some considerable time ago now, the real reception party didn't get going until the couple had left for their honeymoon. This is no longer the case. Most couples stay until the end of the evening and are to be found sharing breakfast with their nearest and dearest the following morning. Honeymoons are usually delayed for a day or so until everything settles down. I can't help thinking this is a welcome innovation. I must say I felt rather cheated to be whisked away from my reception just as things were 'hotting up'.

Honeymoon destinations are usually kept secret and it is always a good idea to keep the 'getaway' vehicle out of sight just in case someone has planned any pranks that may involve decorations that local constabularies might disapprove of.

It would be foolish of me to offer advice here assuming that couples have no intimate knowledge of each other before their marriage. Some of you may have been living together for some time now, or have children to consider.

However, the commitment you have made will change things somewhat. It is often a sobering thought to have made these vows in the sight of God and before so many friends and family. There is much riding on your success as a couple. Please don't be daunted by the expectations of others. Even when things get difficult, keep the channels of communication open. You haven't gone through all of this to stumble at the first hurdle. Everyone who cares for you both and has been part of your day wants your marriage to be a long and happy one; don't be afraid to ask for help when you feel the need. There are few things between lovers and good friends that cannot be worked out with God's help.

If you have not been a regular attender at your local church then what better time to begin than now. You will find that the support and love that the minister and fellowship can offer you as a newly married couple will be invaluable. To say nothing of potential babysitters, should they be required.

Appendices

1. Civil Requirements

Contact the registrar of births, deaths and marriages in the district in which your wedding is to take place as soon as you have fixed a date. He or she will guide you through the process, give you the forms you need to fill in and tell you what type of documentation you will need to provide. Most registrars can send you a pack containing all the information you will need.

It may be if one of you is not a British Citizen then you will have to apply for a marriage visa. Other documents you may require are as follows:

- **birth certificates**
- **divorce documentation**
- **death certificate of previous spouse**

If you are not in possession of any of the required certificates, they can be obtained, in most cases, on-line or by post but be warned: this does take time. If you anticipate any complications then the sooner you take advice from the registrar the better.

In normal circumstances, documentation is not required until about four weeks (six weeks if you are divorced) before the date of the wedding. The **Marriage Schedule** cannot be collected until seven days before the wedding is to take place. There is a fee for this document.

Please check the Schedule carefully and make sure it is kept in a safe place. **It is not possible to conduct a wedding in Scotland unless the Schedule is available at the service.**

The registrar will expect one or other of you to collect this document in person.

(THE WEBSITE OF THE GENERAL REGISTER OFFICE FOR SCOTLAND CONTAINS LOTS OF USEFUL INFORMATION. SEE WWW.GRO-SCOTLAND. CO.UK.)

2. Checklist

- Decide on date and time.
- Confirm date and time with minister/priest and reception venue.
- Contact registrar to check documentation required and timescale.
- Organise rehearsal with the minister.
- Return marriage notices to registrar (four or six weeks beforehand).
- Collect Marriage Schedule from registrar.
- Take Marriage Schedule to minister.

3. Sample Order of Service

Processional Music: Entry of Bridal Party

Welcome and Introduction

Hymn

Prayers

Bible Reading

Exchange of Vows

Exchange of Rings

Declaration of Marriage

Marriage Blessing

Words of Counsel

Reading 2 (if wanted)

Prayers

Hymn

Blessing for all present

Signing of the Schedule (Musical interlude)

Recessional Music: Bride and Groom leave the Church, followed in procession by attendants.

4. Vows

Some suggestions:

Before God
and in the presence
of our families
and friends,
I, A ...
declare my love
for you, B ...
and I give myself to you
as your husband/wife.
I promise you my love
my loyalty and my trust
for as long as we shall both live.

I, A ...
take you, B ...
to be my wife/husband.
In the presence of God
and before this congregation,
I promise and covenant
to be a loving,
faithful, and loyal wife/husband to you
as long as we both shall live.

5. Readings

There are a number of websites that will offer secular readings suitable for weddings. Here is just a small selection of possible Bible readings. Remember, there are lots of different translations of the Bible to choose from and you can decide in advance which verses you wish to have read. Your minister can advise you further.

From the Old Testament

    Genesis 2:15, 18–25
    Song of Solomon 2
    Song of Solomon 8:6–7
    Psalm 67 (a selection of verses)

From the New Testament

    1 Corinthians 13 (all of this or a selection of verses)
    Philippians 1:9–11
    Mark 10:6–9
    John 2:1–11
    John 15:9–12

6. Hymns

These are my choices from the wide range contained in the Fourth Version of the Church Hymnary, each of which has a well-known tune. There are many other books available. If you don't want to have the hymns printed out (this may involve copyright issues) then check which books are available at the church.

462	The King of Love
519	Love Divine
695	Your love, O God, has called us here
696	We come, dear Lord, to celebrate
697	Let's praise the Creator
698	The grace of life is theirs
699	God beyond Glory
700	As man and woman

7. Prayer/Meditation

I include a prayer that you may wish to reflect upon together.

Circle us Lord,
with bright gifts of compassion
of tolerance and of forgiveness.
Surround us Lord,
with your joy and all-encompassing love
that we might love each other
with warm and welcoming hearts.
Enfold us Lord,
that together we can embrace the future
with faithful constancy and delight,
in the name of Jesus Christ
who showed us all how to live
and how to love.
AMEN